From the desktops of Andy and Gil Leaf

One of the most important lessons our father taught us is the value of reading. The exhilaration of turning a page and having words leap out, begging to be uttered and embraced, is a profound experience that is permanently etched in the mind. A book expands horizons, and from reading comes wisdom. This was his message to every child. A springboard for the imagination, a book can be educational *and* fun.

It is a huge joy that the key to the amusing, creative, and engaging world of our father can once again be found on bookshelves. He would be tremendously pleased and satisfied to know that today, sixty-five years and one century later, his words still have resonance—words that will be fondly remembered by generations past, and words that will be savored, chuckled over, and read countless times by a new generation of curious, inquisitive, and impressionable young eyes.

Your Name Here

BRUSHING YOUR TEETH CAN BE FUN

First published in the United States of America in 2008
by UNIVERSE PUBLISHING
A Division of Rizzoli International Publications, Inc.
300 Park Avenue South
New York, NY 10010
www.rizzoliusa.com

Originally published as *Health Can Be Fun*
© 1943 Munro Leaf

2008 2009 2010 2011 2012 / 10 9 8 7 6 5 4 3 2 1

Printed in China

ISBN 10: 0-7893-1594-7
ISBN 13: 978-0-7893-1594-6

Library of Congress Catalog Control Number: 2007904938

Cover design: Headcase Design
www.headcasedesign.com

BRUSHING YOUR TEETH CAN BE FUN

AND LOTS OF OTHER GOOD IDEAS FOR HOW TO GROW UP HEALTHY, STRONG, AND SMART

Munro Leaf

UNIVERSE

GOOD HEALTH

is something we don't think

about very much

until

WE

DON'T

HAVE

IT.

Then, when we

are sick and

feel awful, we

promise ourselves

that we will take

better care of our

HEALTH

as soon as we get well.

BUT

when we do feel better

again, too many of us

just forget all about

it.

That is a foolish way to

behave and as

long as we act

like that we shall probably

keep right on being

sick or weak or wobbly

a lot of the time.

BECAUSE

**STAYING
HEALTHY**

is a game we

have to play all

the time,

not just once in a

while.

When we are

BABIES

Somebody has to see that

we have the right

food and clothes

and that we get
exercise and fresh air

that we are kept clean

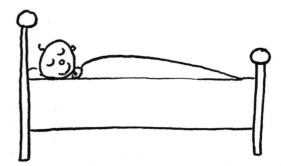

and have enough
rest and sleep.

SOMEBODY ELSE HAS TO TAKE
CARE OF ALL THAT FOR US

But—

As we grow older and bigger we learn

more and more

until after a while

we know how

to take care of ourselves.

We know why we must

drink some things and

eat some things

to make our bodies

grow

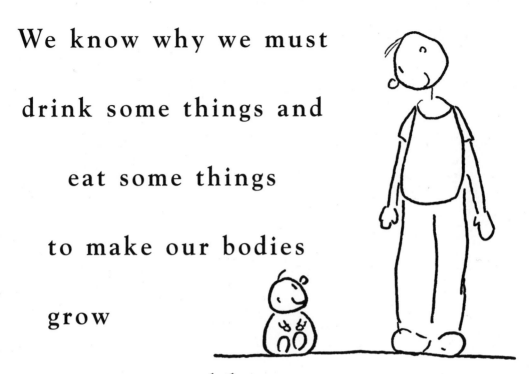

stronger and better.

First

We find out about the

we drink.

It comes from cows

and it is the best food or
drink for us that
anybody has ever found
anywhere in the world.
Milk has in it more different things
than any other single food or drink
that will
build strong muscles
and
good bones and teeth
and
give us energy and pep
all at the same time.

It has sugar and fats that we need and
vitamins that help to keep us well.
Milk is a food that costs so little and

gives us so much that we can see why
the best doctors tell us that we should
drink at least three cups of it every day.
When we KNOW things like that
we don't have to have people
nag at us and scold and beg to get us
to drink milk.

But we know too that as good as
milk is for us, it still isn't enough.

We couldn't get along as growing

boys and girls on just milk alone.

We need to eat bread and meat, fish

and eggs,

fresh vegetables, fruits,

cereals and other foods to

build strong, healthy bodies.

And if there is one creature
that makes everybody tired
it's a

FOOD GRUMBLER

that

won't eat what

is good for it—

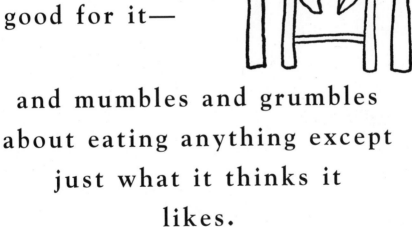

and mumbles and grumbles
about eating anything except
just what it thinks it
likes.

Even when we eat the same food, all of us don't grow to be the same size and shape.

Some of us are tall, some short, some heavier than others and some lighter. But all of us don't want to do the same things and be exactly alike, so it is a good thing that we are different.

We do want to be well and

healthy though, so that no matter what

size we are or what we do,

we can be

helpful to others and happy

ourselves.

EXERCISE

One of the best ways to keep ourselves

healthy is to get plenty of good

exercise.

To move around out in the fresh air

every day, working

and playing,

is the best way to stretch muscles

and make them grow.

Boys and girls who just sit around

all the time are never as healthy

as others and they don't

have as much fun

either.

If you just flop and mope around
like a lump, and never run or
jump or ride or walk fast with
your head up and your shoulders
back, you will miss a lot.
And don't be surprised if you grow up

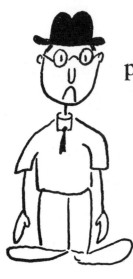to be a dull soggy
person who is about
as much fun to
be with as a bag
of wet sand.

Whatever kind of exercise you take at

work or play try to remember that

you will be a lot

more comfortable, healthy, and better

looking if you aren't a

STOOPER

that walks around with its shoulders so

bent over it looks like a monkey—

or a SLOUCHER

that sits down as though its seat were

up in the middle of its back.

REST AND SLEEP

One of the most important things
we have to do to stay healthy
is to get enough
REST

Workers know it
Soldiers know it
Sailors know it
and even animals know it.

But—

Some Boys   and Girls

who should know that we

need to rest the most while we are

still growing

Scream and yell

or

Moan and groan

or

pout and whine

like tiny babies when it is

time to take a

nap or go to bed

at night.

That makes more people

angry than almost

anything else that silly

children do.

It is as bad manners to

cry and argue about going

to bed when we should

as it is unhealthy.

 So

GO TO BED

when you should

and STOP fussing about it

like a two-year-old.

When you sleep

be sure that you have some

fresh air in your room.

That doesn't mean you have to freeze

the place and have drafts blowing

through it, but it needs to be well aired

and ventilated for the best sleeping.

KEEPING
CLEAN
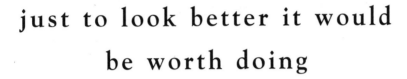
if we
kept ourselves
clean
just to look better it would
be worth doing
But
there are more important reasons
than that for
keeping ourselves clean.
DIRT and GERMS that

make us
sick
go together
and
WORK TOGETHER

IF WE
WANT TO STAY HEALTHY
AND WELL

WE HAVE TO WASH
OURSELVES
REGULARLY

NOT JUST

SOAP

WASH CLOTH

OUR FACES

BUT

Our Hands

most of all

and

all the rest

of our

bodies

sometimes.

DO YOU KNOW WHY?

Because

in all dirt there are GERMS.

They are tiny live things, so

little we can't even see them,

 unless we look at them

through a microscope,

but they are there just the same.

Some Germs are Disease Germs

that make us sick if they get

inside us.

They get into us mostly through

our mouths and noses,

but they can go in through

our skin too.

SO

if we keep ourselves clean

and get the dirt off us

the germs have less

chance to get inside.

When we eat we often touch
the food that goes inside us
and if our hands are full
of dirt and germs, even if we
can't see them, there they go
right into our mouths.

That is why we always
try to wash our hands before
we eat.

And just count how many
times you put your hands up
to your mouth and nose
and you will see why
it makes good sense to
keep them clean.

BATHS

Make us clean all over

on the outside

And we must

not forget

that

It is just as important for

us to be clean

INSIDE

If we are to stay healthy

and well.

The FOOD we eat
gets all divided up inside
us.
Some of it goes to make
muscle and to build our
bodies bigger and stronger.
Some goes to make teeth and
strengthen our bones, some
for hair and fingernails and
toenails and all parts of us.
The part of the food that
isn't any good for us and
is just waste goes on
through our bodies and
we get rid of it.

That is why we go to the
toilet.
If this old waste food stayed
inside us too long it would
make us sick too.
So it is very important that
at least once every day we
go to the toilet to get rid
of this old waste food.
And remember this.
After we have gone to the toilet
We should be very
sure to WASH
OUR HANDS

TEETH

We get two sets of teeth,

and we need to take good care of them

First we get our

Baby teeth.

One or two at a time.

These usually start to come when

we are about six or eight months old.

We get our four big back

teeth

and as our grown-up teeth come

in our front baby teeth come

out.

It is very important for us
to keep our teeth clean
so they will be healthy
and not decay.
If we take good care of our first
baby teeth, then our grown-up
teeth will come in straighter and
stronger.
Then we have to be sure to
keep our grown-up teeth
well cleaned because
they are the last
ones we will ever
get.
Nobody ever gets more than two sets
of real teeth. So
Take Care of them.

Be Sure

To brush them

in the morning and every night

before you go to bed.

Many people think it is

very wise to brush

them after every meal.

If you have a dentist look at

your teeth twice every year, you

won't have so many toothaches

and you will keep your

teeth longer.

HAIR AND FINGERNAILS

Our hair and our fingernails

need to be kept clean

and cut

unless YOU

WANT TO BE A MESSY

AND

LOOK LIKE ONE.

And don't forget your
Toenails, just
because they happen
to be hidden by your
socks and shoes in the daytime.

CLOTHES

The clothes we wear have
a lot to do with our
health.

Clean clothes are healthy clothes.

It won't do us very much good to

take a bath if we put dirty

clothes back on us.

Some people are just too lazy
to change their clothes as
often as they should
and somebody has to nag

at them all the time to
make them do it.
That gets tiresome and anybody
with any real sense would change his
or her clothes without all that squawking—
and everybody would feel better.

When it is cold we wear
more clothes to keep us
warm.
That is simple and almost
anybody can understand
why we do that.
BUT
the thing just as simple that a lot of
people don't seem to understand is that
it is just as dangerous to be too warm
as it is to be too cold.

When we come into heated houses in the winter we should take off the heavy clothes that we wear outdoors.

If we don't we get too warm and the next time we go out, we are very likely to catch a cold.

More people are sick from catching COLDS than from any other disease. We catch them by breathing in the germs that are spread by other people who have colds, or from getting chilled after being too warm, or sitting

or sleeping in a draft or getting our shoes or clothes wet and cold and not changing them soon enough.

If we take care to stay away
from people who sneeze and cough
and if we dress sensibly
and wear rubber boots or overshoes
when there is rain or snow
we are not so likely to
catch colds.
When we do catch a cold
then is the time we should
take extra good care of
ourselves.

First
We want to get well ourselves
because it is no
fun to have a cold
and
Second
We don't want to give them
to other people.
To get well ourselves there
are so many things we can
do to make us feel better,
but the most important
is to STAY IN BED AND
REST FOR AT LEAST ONE
WHOLE DAY AND NIGHT.

Just having a cold by itself
isn't so very dangerous
and if we take good
care of ourselves we can usually
be well in about seven or nine days.
BUT the
reason we have to be so careful
is that when we have a cold
we are very likely to
catch some other kind
of disease.
Colds make us weaker than we usually
are and if we don't do what we
should we may catch
something else and be
sick for a
long time.

So

if you feel hot and stuffy and
your nose is runny, and you
start to sneeze or cough

Don't keep it a secret.

Tell the people who

take care of you and

do the right things

to get rid of it as

soon as you can.

While you are sneezing or coughing

be sure to cover your
nose and mouth so that
you won't spread your

Cold Germs for other people to breathe.
Nobody is going to thank you for giving
him or her a cold.

 **CUTS**   **SCRATCHES**

BURNS   **BLISTERS**

and

POISON IVY.

There are lots of little things that happen to us all the time like getting scratched or cut or raising a blister,  catching poison ivy or being stung by mosquitoes that raise bumps on us. For every one of these there is a right and a wrong thing to do and your job is to let grown-ups know what has happened to you so they

50

can be sure you get the

right care.

We don't know enough about

medicine to be sure which

ones we should use

 for what.

But

Those of us who are smart

know that we should tell

others when something

is wrong with us.

Sometimes we need to
see a doctor.

Doctors are people who
have studied and worked
a long time to learn
how to make us
well again when we are
sick.
They know better than we do
what we should do.
So if
we are wise we learn to
know our Doctors as
our friends and do
what they tell us to when
they are helping us.

Some anxious people think that
staying healthy is a
sad and gloomy thing.
They sit around and
mope and worry about
how they feel all the
time.
When they feel all right
they worry because they
are afraid they won't
be well the next day.
That is just plain
Silly and Foolish.

STAYING HEALTHY

is
a
game
we
play
all the time.
Being smart
and
using
our
brains
to do
the
simple, right things
every day
will keep us
STRONG and HAPPY

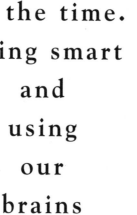

because

BRUSHING YOUR TEETH
CAN BE FUN.